Christ. 1971

Geoffrey,

with love,

John, Margaret. Cub and Alexander

Cartier Discovers the St Lawrence

By William Toye

Illustrated by Laszlo Gal

LONDON OXFORD UNIVERSITY PRESS 1971

Oxford University Press, Ely House, London W.1

GLASGOW NEW YORK TORONTO MELBOURNE WELLINGTON CAPE TOWN SALISBURY IBADAN NAIROBI DAR ES SALAAM LUSAKA ADDIS ABABA
BOMBAY CALCUTTA MADRAS KARACHI LAHORE DACCA KUALA LUMPUR SINGAPORE HONG KONG TOKYO

©Oxford University Press (Canadian Branch) 1970   Printed in Italy by Arnoldo Mondadori

Labrador
Strait of Belle Isle
Anticosti Island
Gaspé
New-found-Land
Chaleur Bay
Cape Indian
Cape Breton Island
The First Voyage

The First Voyage

In the early sixteenth century when Jacques Cartier was growing up in France, Europeans thought that by sailing across the Atlantic to the West they could reach Asia, the land of silks and spices. Columbus thought he had reached the East Indies when he made his landfall in 1492. John Cabot thought he had reached Asia when he touched the mainland of America in 1497.

With other voyages westward, and as more and more fishermen went to the Grand Banks off Newfoundland, men came to believe that if the great land mass that had been discovered in the West — what we call North America — was not Asia, at least a route might be found through it that would lead to the riches of the East.

Jacques Cartier was born in 1491 in the coastal town of St Malo, France. He was a navigator who may already have been to the New World when in 1534 he was fitted to sail for the king, Francis I, "to discover certain islands and lands where it is said that a great quantity of gold and other precious things are to be found." It was also hoped that he would find the route to Asia. He set out from St Malo in April in two ships manned by a crew of sixty-one.

An account of two of his three voyages has been left to us in the form of a journal. Cartier no doubt kept a logbook, but the records we know were likely put down by some unknown writer who heard of the voyages from Cartier's own lips.

Stiff winds, blowing fresh and strong from the east, carried the tiny vessels across the Atlantic in twenty days. The first land they sighted was Cape Bonavista on the east coast of Newfoundland: they sailed around the northern tip of the island into the heavy gales that roared through the strait separating Newfoundland from Labrador (the Strait of Belle Isle). Cartier gingerly steered his course past the gigantic icebergs that were moving eastward to the ocean. Then, on the forbidding coast of Labrador ("the land God gave to Cain", he called it), he saw people.

They wear their hair tied up on the top of their heads like a handful of twisted hay, with a nail or something of the sort passed through the middle, and into it they weave a few birds' feathers. They clothe themselves with the furs of animals, both men as well as women... They paint themselves with certain tan colours. They *have canoes made of birchbark in which they go about and from which they catch many seals.*

Cartier sailed down the west coast of Newfoundland for nine days. Northeasterly winds blew cold and hard; the weather was dark. All he could see of Newfoundland through the fog was a gloomy vista of harsh mountains.

He turned southwest in the Gulf of St Lawrence to search for the passage to China, and he came upon many green islands that delighted him after the stern prospect of Labrador and Newfoundland. One was "covered with fine trees and meadows, fields of wild oats, and of pease in flower, as thick and as fine as ever I saw in Brittany..." Like the master mariner he was, he carefully charted his course through this labyrinth of islands and false bays, taking soundings and studying the characteristics of the land he was seeing for the first time.

He discovered Prince Edward Island without knowing it was an island, naming the north-western tip Cape Indian.

At this cape a man came in sight who ran after our longboats along the coast, making frequent signs to us to return towards the said point. And seeing these signs we began to row towards him, but when he saw that we were returning, he started to run away and to flee before us. We landed opposite to him and placed a knife and a woollen girdle on a branch and then returned to our ships.

He explored the west coast of the island for a few miles in search of a harbour — unsuccessfully, for the shore was low and the water shallow. Then he headed north. His hopes were raised when he entered a bay whose great width and depth suggested that here might be a passage like the Strait of Belle Isle, possibly one that would lead to the other side of the continent. He anchored his ships in a cove and set out in one of the longboats to see in what direction the coast ran.

His men had been rowing for half a league (about a mile and a half) when forty or fifty canoes glided into view filled with painted, chattering Micmacs. They had been fishing for

mackerel and were crossing from one side of the bay to the other. When they reached shore they sprang out of their canoes and started to shout and yell, beckoning all the while to the Frenchmen and waving some pelts on the ends of sticks. "We did not care to go," Cartier's journal says, for the Frenchmen mistrusted such a large band of Indians. But the natives were not discouraged. They got back into their canoes, keeping up their uproarious sounds of welcome, and began to surround the white men in the water. Cartier's efforts to shoo them off were futile, so he shot two small cannon in the air and two fire lances (long sticks filled with

powder). For a moment the Indians were stunned; then, howling in surprise and terror, they hastily paddled off.

But the chief did not remain cowed for long. The next day he led another fleet of canoes to Cartier's ships and the Indians made signs that they had come to barter. This time Cartier relaxed towards them. He sent two men to meet them and give them knives and hatchets and a red cap to their delighted chief. Then trading started in earnest, and while it went on some of the Indians danced on the shore and threw water over their heads in their excitement.

Cartier finally came upon the head of the bay they had been exploring. It did not after all lead to a passage through the continent, a discovery that "grieved and displeased" them all. But he observed that the land there was fair, "as full of beautiful fields and meadows as any we have ever seen", and that the water was as level as a pond as it sparkled under the blazing summer sun. He named the bay Chaleur—Bay of Heat.

Seeing there was no passage, we proceeded to turn back. While making our way along the shore we caught sight of the Indians on the side of a lagoon and low beach, who were making many fires that smoked. We rowed over to the spot, and finding there was an entrance from the sea into the lagoon, we placed our longboats on one side of the entrance. The savages came over in one of their canoes and brought us some strips of cooked seal, which they placed on bits of wood and then withdrew, making signs to us that they were making us a present of them. We sent two men on shore with hatchets, knives, beads and other wares, at which the Indians showed great pleasure. And at once they came over in a crowd in their canoes to the side where we were, bringing furs and whatever else they possessed, in order to obtain some of our wares. They numbered, both men, women and children, more than 300 persons. Some of their women, who did not come over, danced and sang, standing in the water up to their knees. The other women, who had come over to the side where we were, advanced freely towards us and rubbed our arms with their hands. Then they joined their hands together and raised them to heaven, exhibiting many signs of joy. And so much at ease did the savages feel in our presence that at length we bartered with them, hand to hand, for everything they possessed, so that nothing was left to them but their naked bodies; for they offered us everything they owned, which was all told of little value.

Nine days were spent in Gaspé Harbour sheltered from the wind and mist of the Gulf that prevented further passage north. On Gaspé Peninsula, in the presence of a number of Indians from Stadacona,* Cartier raised a thirty-foot wooden cross bearing the shield of France with three fleur-de-lys and above it on a wooden board the words VIVE LE ROY DE FRANCE ("Long Live the King of France"). Most of the Indians were impressed when the men knelt before the cross, but the chief was not.

When we had returned to our ships, the chief, dressed in an old black bear-skin, arrived in a canoe with three of his sons and his brother; but they did not come so close to the ships as they had usually done. And pointing to the cross he made us a long harangue, making the sign of the cross with two of his fingers; and then he pointed to the land all around about, as if he wished to say that all this region belonged to him, and that we ought not to have set up this cross without his permission. And when he had finished his harangue, we held up an axe to him, pretending we would barter it for his fur-skin. To this he nodded assent and little by little drew near the side of our vessel, thinking he would have the axe. But one of our men, who was in our dinghy, caught hold of his canoe, and at once two or three more stepped down into it and made the Indians come on

board our vessel, at which they were greatly astonished. When they had come on board, they were assured by the captain [Cartier] that no harm would befall them, while at the same time every sign of affection was shown to them; and they were made to eat and to drink and to be of good cheer. And then we explained to them by signs that the cross had been set up to serve as a landmark and guidepost on coming into the harbour, and that we would soon come back and would bring them iron wares and other goods; and that we wished to take two of his sons away with us and afterwards would bring them back again to that harbour. And we dressed up his two sons [Taignoagny and Dom Agaya] in shirts and ribbons and in red caps, and put a little brass chain around the neck of each, at which they were greatly pleased; and they proceeded to hand over their old rags to those who were going back on shore. To each of these three, whom we sent back, we also gave a hatchet and two knives at which they showed great pleasure. When they had returned on shore, they told the others what had happened. About noon on that day six canoes came off to the ships, in each of which were five or six Indians, who had come to say goodbye to the two we had detained, and to bring them some fish. These made signs to us that they would not pull down the cross, delivering at the same time several harangues which we did not understand.

Cartier and his men then sailed to the northwest tip of Anticosti Island where there came into view an irresistible sight that beckoned them to proceed — a great expanse of water stretching westward to infinity. Excitement and curiosity drove them on. They got into their longboats, and with thirteen oars rowed furiously against the violent tide. But they made no headway. Heavy east winds had set in. The summer was more than half over and the tides were getting stronger; further exploration was perilous. Should they try to proceed in the waters that foamed so angrily to the west or should they turn homeward? The crew had a meeting. They dare not, they decided, chance being trapped there for the winter. So they voted to return to France.

Cartier left by way of the Strait of Belle Isle in early August, having become the first European navigator to record a circuit of the Gulf of St Lawrence.

We do not know what his reception was when he arrived in France in September. He did not bring with him any gold or gems and this caused disappointment in some quarters. But he did have natives from the New World. Taignoagny and Dom Agaya must have excited much curiosity, particularly when they learned French well enough to speak of a mysterious "Kingdom of Saguenay". Cartier had also glimpsed what looked like a sea off Anticosti Island. The Kingdom (could it be another treasure-filled Mexico such as the Spaniards had found?) and the existence of a great open expanse of water (where does it lead?) gave hint of marvels to be discovered and exploited. They were enough to enlist the king's help for a second voyage.

The Second Voyage

On May 16, 1535, Cartier joined a new crew in the cathedral of St Malo. There each man confessed himself, took communion, and received the bishop's blessing. On May 19 they set sail.

Cartier had three ships this time: the *Grande Hermine* (120 tons), on which he sailed, the *Petite Hermine* (60 tons), and the *Emérillon* (40 tons). On board were provisions for fifteen months and a company of 112 people, including the brothers Taignoagny and Dom Agaya. The ships were parted from each other in mid-Atlantic by furious gales from the west and by dense fogs, but they met again, more than two months later, in the Strait of Belle Isle.

They spent the feast day of St Lawrence sheltered in a bay on the north shore of the Gulf opposite Anticosti Island, and Cartier named this bay after the saint, whose name later came to be applied to the whole gulf and even to the river that lay waiting to be discovered. When the winds died down three days later they explored the south (Gaspé) shore and then sailed further along the north shore to make sure no strait existed there before continuing westward.

Taignoagny and Dom Agaya were approaching familiar territory and could answer Cartier's questions about it.

The two Indians assured us that this was the way to the mouth of the great river of Hochelaga and the route towards Canada, and that the river grew narrower as one approached Canada; and also that farther up the water became fresh, and that one could make one's way so far up the river that they had never heard of anyone reaching the head of it.

"Canada" was the name the Indians gave to a region along the river some forty miles east and west of Stadacona.

The river had been entered now, and not powerful tidal currents, nor sandbars, nor hidden reefs could turn them from their course. The ships neared the mouth of the Saguenay where this towering chasm pours its inky waters into the St Lawrence, and the sailors caught sight of four canoes filled with Indians fishing. The natives were frightened and drew near to the ships fearfully, until Taignoagny called out to them in their native tongue; then they came alongside.

The Frenchmen glided further and further into a gradually narrowing river-world. The air they breathed became heavy with the pungent aroma of pine and cedar. No human appeared to them; nothing but bird-calls broke the stillness of the vast mountain wilderness that stretched on either side of them.

They came to some islands, on one of which grapes grew so plentifully that the sailors named it Isle of Bacchus in honour of the Greek god of wine. (Cartier called it the Isle of Orleans.) They cast anchor between this island and the north shore.

The next day a chief named Donnacona appeared.

And when he was opposite to the smallest of our three ships, this chief began to make a speech and to harangue us, moving his body and his limbs in a marvellous manner, as is their custom when showing joy and contentment. And when he came opposite to the Captain's vessel, on board of which were Taignoagny and Dom Agaya, the chief spoke to them and they to him, telling him what they had seen in France, and the good treatment meted out to them there. At this the chief was much pleased and begged the Captain to stretch out his arms to him that he might hug and kiss them, which is the way they welcome one in that country.

About thirty miles upstream they reached a river that Cartier called the Ste Croix (now the St Charles). It runs into the St Lawrence near a high cliff on top of which was the village of Stadacona where Donnacona lived. The smallest ship, the *Emérillon*, was left at anchor out in the St Lawrence to continue the journey upstream while the two larger ships were moored in the Ste Croix.

The Indians told Cartier of another village, called Hochelaga, that stood further upriver. Cartier was determined to see it and announced that he would go there. But Donnacona and Taignoagny were not in favour of this, as though they didn't want to share the white men and their trade goods with the tribes to the

west. They refused to go with him, saying that the river was not worth exploring.

Cartier ignored this opposition, so the natives tried to frighten him into staying with them. On a Saturday morning, as the Frenchmen were preparing to depart, they saw moving towards their ship a canoe bearing three monstrous figures. They were covered in black-and-white dogskin and had black faces; horns seemed to protrude from their heads. One of them shouted something at Cartier and all three collapsed as if dead in the bottom of the canoe. Then Taignoagny and Dom Agaya rushed out of the woods and made motions and sounds of terror.

Taignoagny began to speak and repeated three times "Jesus! Jesus! Jesus", lifting his eyes towards heaven. Then Dom Agaya called out "Jesus! Maria! Jacques Cartier!", looking up to heaven as the other had done. The Captain, seeing their grimaces and gesticulations, began to ask them what was the matter and what new event had happened? They replied that there was bad news, adding that indeed it was far from good. The Captain again asked them what was the trouble. They answered that their god, Cudouagny by name, had made an announcement at Hochelaga and that the three above-mentioned Indians had come in his name to tell them the tidings, which were that there would be so much ice and snow that all would perish. At this we all began to laugh and to tell them that their god was a mere fool who did not know what he was saying; and that they should tell his messengers as much; and that Jesus would keep them safe from the cold if they would trust in him.

Taignoagny and Dom Agaya, "who were altogether changed in their attitude and good will", then told Cartier that Donnacona would not let them go with him to Hochelaga unless Cartier left behind a hostage. Cartier replied that if they would not go willingly they could stay, that he had no intention of giving up his plan to reach Hochelaga on their account.

The next day the *Emérillon* continued slowly up the St Lawrence with the tide. "Along both shores we had sight of the finest and most beautiful land it is possible to see," the journal says, "being as level as a pond and covered with the most magnificent trees in the world." These trees were turning, and the forest on either side of the ship was ablaze with red and gold. Every few miles friendly Indians came to the shore to welcome the Frenchmen with shouting and dancing and to give them fish or whatever else they possessed in exchange for trinkets. None seemed alarmed or surprised by the appearance of the strange craft.

When the ship was grounded in shallow water, they continued upstream in two long-boats towards Hochelaga, over a thousand miles inland from the ocean they had crossed. They arrived three days later, on October 2, coming ashore at a place where "there is the most violent rapid it is possible to see, which we were unable to pass".

And on reaching Hochelaga there came to meet us more than a thousand persons — men, women and children — who gave us as good a welcome as ever father gave to his son, making great signs of joy; for the men danced in one

ring, the women in another and the children also apart by themselves. After this they brought us quantities of fish and of their bread which is made of Indian corn, throwing so much of it into our longboats that it seemed to rain bread. Seeing this the Captain, accompanied by several of his men, went on shore; and no sooner had he landed than they all crowded about him and about the others, giving them a wonderful reception. And the women brought their babies in their arms to have the Captain and his companions touch them, while all held a merry-making which lasted more than half an hour. Seeing their generosity and friendli-

ness, the Captain had the women all sit down in a row and gave them some tin beads and other trifles; and to some of the men he gave knives. Then he returned on board the longboats to sup and pass the night.

Darkness fell. The Indians lighted huge bonfires on shore and in the flickering firelight they danced some more, their jumping, jiggling bodies vying with the leaping flames. And as they danced they shouted their greeting and exclamation of joy — "Aguyase! Aguyase!" Rhythmically, monotonously it echoed across the river all through the night.

18

The next day Cartier put on his armour and with three Indian guides led his party on a march to Hochelaga. Oak trees towered above them with leaves turned brown; the path they walked on was covered with acorns. Presently they came upon cultivated land, open fields of maize (Indian corn). In the middle of the fields stood the village of Hochelaga surrounded by palisades — upright trunks set in a triple row — and behind it the great hill that Cartier named Mount Royal.

Cartier entered the village through the single gate. Inside he saw fifty oblong houses made of sapling poles covered with large sheets of bark. Each dwelling contained many rooms and housed several families. In the centre of the village was a square where Cartier and his men received the excited natives. The women surrounded the party as before, touching the Frenchmen's faces and weeping for joy; the Indian men, after making the women retire, sat on the ground around them, row upon row, "as if we had been going to perform a play". Then the chief was carried in on a deerskin. Though not an old man, he was paralysed. He showed his arms and legs to Cartier, signalling him to touch them as if he expected to be cured. Other sick people came forward — the blind, the lame, the deformed — hopeful that some kind of miracle could be performed by the white man. Cartier was touched by this demonstration of faith. He felt that a ceremony was called for and read to them from the Gospel of St John, made the sign of the cross over the sick, and prayed aloud for them. The Indians listened gravely to his every word, "looking up to heaven and imitating us in gestures".

Finally Cartier presented hatchets and knives to the men, beads to the women, and objects of tin to the children. And as a final treat called for a blast on the trumpets which delighted the Indians greatly.

Cartier then climbed slowly to the top of Mount Royal, followed by a crowd of men and women. From the summit he could see more than ninety miles of the surrounding country glowing with autumn colours. He saw mountains to the north and another range to the south and level land between, broken by the broad silver river that ran through it as far as the eye could see.

The Indians told Cartier of the Ottawa River. Pointing to the silver whistle he wore round his neck and to the gilt handle of a dagger that looked like gold, they signalled that these metals were to be found to the north. They were shown a piece of copper. This metal,

they said, was found in the Kingdom of Saguenay.

They all went back down the mountain together. It was a long walk at the end of a tiring day and the sailors stumbled with fatigue. Seeing this, the Indians heaved the shorter Frenchmen on their shoulders and carried them pig-a-back until the longboats were finally reached. Later, as Cartier glided away from them, the Indians of Hochelaga followed the boats as far as they could along the shore, regretting to see the last of him.

The men who remained on the river Ste Croix had worked hard. They had built a tim-

ber fort with palisades in which the ships' cannons had been set at intervals facing all directions; the two ships themselves were moored before it.

Donnacona seemed glad when Cartier returned. He invited him to visit his village of Stadacona. Again the Frenchmen were warmly welcomed by the natives, who ran out to meet them as the party approached their bark houses. The men seated themselves in a row on one side of the white men and the girls stood on the other singing and dancing. After gifts were distributed — knives to the men and a tin ring to each of the women who passed in procession to receive it — Cartier was shown round. He saw inside some houses in which food was stored for the winter. He was asked to admire five enemy scalps stretched on hoops and Donnacona told Cartier some amazing things about the Kingdom of Saguenay to the northwest.

"The natives wear woollen clothes as the

white men do," he said. "There are many towns and tribes made up of good people who have much gold and copper."

Cartier also heard about a land of fruit trees far to the south where there was never any ice or snow. He took this to be somewhere near Florida.

A month passed. The air became crisp and snowflakes began to fall. A numbing wind blew up. Soon the river froze and all the land was covered with snow, more than four feet of it. Ice locked the ships into the harbour and snow-drifts rose around them as high as the bulwarks. The Indians alone seemed unaffected by the cold; they strode calmly into the drifts half naked.

In December scurvy broke out in Stadacona. The winter diet of the Indians brought it on and more than fifty natives died; even Dom Agaya was stricken. Then the white men, who were without fresh food and had eaten too much salt pork, succumbed to the disease. Cartier's journal describes how

some lost all their strength, their legs became swollen and inflamed, while the sinews contracted and turned black as coal. . . . And all had their mouths so tainted that the gums rotted away down to the roots of the teeth, which nearly all fell out.

By the middle of February there were not ten men of the 112 who had escaped the disease. Eight had died and another fifty seemed near death. The dead had to be buried in snow-drifts for the ground was frozen hard.

Mercifully Cartier remained in good health, but he was powerless to check the onslaught of the disease or do anything but watch helplessly as his men died one by one. In desperation he gave orders for all to pray for assistance. He had an image of the Virgin nailed to a tree, and a procession of gaunt, disease-ridden men — all who could walk — stumbled painfully through the snow, singing psalms and litanies, to kneel before it and pray.

On top of the sickness Cartier was worried about the Indians, for they were ominously silent. He did not trust them. He feared that if they discovered the feeble condition of his company they might attack them. He tried to mislead them by having some of his men make banging noises to suggest activity on the ships; and whenever Indians came within sight, he appeared on the ice with two or three well men and pretended to beat them as though driving them back to the ships to work with the others.

One day Cartier met Dom Agaya, whom he had seen nearly two weeks before ravaged with sickness, completely restored to normal.

"How were you cured?" asked Cartier, overjoyed to see that recovery was possible.

"I have been healed by the juice and dregs of some leaves," Dom Agaya replied. "That is the only way to cure the sickness."

"Where can we find these leaves?" Cartier asked. Quickly he added: "I want to cure my servant," for he was afraid to reveal the extent of the epidemic among his sailors.

Dom Agaya sent two squaws to gather some cedar branches. They showed Cartier how to grind the bark and how to boil it with the leaves. They told him to have the sick man drink it every two days, and to put the dregs on the affected parts of his body.

At first the half-dead men refused to touch such a strange brew. But when one or two tried it and felt better, they all rushed to drink some greedily. Soon after, their health began to improve. They consumed a tall tree in eight days and "it benefited us so much that all who were

willing to use it recovered health and strength, thanks be to God."

The air grew milder. The ice began to melt and the ships floated free. The Stadacona Indians, joined now by other natives that Cartier had never seen before, began to look as though they might attack the white men. Their manner had changed so much that Cartier hastened his plans to leave. First the *Petite Hermine* was scuttled because the crew had been so reduced by disease there were not enough to man it. Cartier had made up his mind to take Don-nacona back to France to tell the king himself of the wonders of the Kingdom of Saguenay — the gold, the rubies, and other rich things, and of the strange one-legged people the chief said lived there. (These were falsehoods, of course. They may have been told to Cartier as a joke or to impress him and excite his interest, for the Indians had a way of telling the Frenchmen what they thought they wanted to hear. Or the Frenchmen might have interpreted the Indians' sign-language to make it mean what they wanted it to mean.)

Early in May, after a cross-planting ceremony on the river-bank, Cartier invited Donnacona to visit him on his ship. As soon as
the old chief set foot in the fort he was
seized, along with Dom Agaya, Taignoagny,
and two other natives. Pandemonium broke
loose as the Indians who had come with them
fled in fear "like sheep before the wolves".
Later the bereft natives reappeared on shore
and called for their chief who was now on board
ship. They began to show signs of violence,
so Cartier had Donnacona speak to them from
the deck.

"The captain is taking me to see his king,"
the chief said. "He has promised to give me a
fine present and to bring me back within ten or
twelve moons."

"Ho! ho! ho!" yelled the Indians, giving their
customary sign of approval and pleasure.

*Then these people and Donnacona made
several harangues and went through various
ceremonies which, as we did not understand
them, it is impossible to describe.*

At daybreak next morning the Indians sent
four squaws in a canoe to the ship (they did
not send men "for fear lest we detain them",
the journal says).

*And Donnacona begged the Captain to say
to them that he would return within twelve
moons, and would bring Donnacona to Canada.
He spoke thus to set their minds at rest. The
Captain did as requested, whereupon the
squaws pretended to be much pleased, and gave
him to understand by signs and words that
should he ever return and bring back Donnacona and the rest, the whole tribe would give
him many presents. After this each of them
offered the Captain a string of wampum. Then
they retired to the opposite bank of the river
[Ste Croix] where the whole population of
Stadacona was collected; and all withdrew
waving farewell to their chief, Donnacona.*

Cartier took a new, shorter route home. He left the Gulf through the passage between Anticosti Island and the Gaspé Peninsula, discovered Cabot Strait, and sailed through it along the south coast of Newfoundland. He entered the ocean on June 19 and reached St Malo on July 16, 1536.

Chief Donnacona's report of the Kingdom of Saguenay, of its minerals and the strange (fictitious) people who lived there, were deeply interesting to the king. But Francis was too occupied with a war with Spain to give any thought just then to sending out an expedition to explore it.

The years passed. The Indians — among them four children who had been given to Cartier at Stadacona—were well treated. Three of them were baptized. But foreign ways did not agree with them and the germs of civilized life took their toll. One by one they died, except for a little girl. What became of her we do not know.

The Third Voyage

In 1541 the king's "dear and beloved Jacques Cartier, who has discovered the large countries of Canada and Hochelaga which lie at the end of Asia", visited the St Lawrence one more time. The king had decided to start a colony in Canada. Only a nobleman could act as his lieutenant-general and he appointed the Sieur de Roberval to lead the expedition. Cartier was therefore in a subordinate position on his third voyage.

Five ships were made ready for him at St Malo, among them the *Grande Hermine* and the *Emérillon*. He sailed with a large crew and some colonists on May 23 — without Roberval, who did not yet have his supplies. Three months later (the passage was a stormy one) Cartier arrived at Stadacona.

Indians came out to meet the ships in great excitement. Agona, the chief who had been appointed by Donnacona, was among them. Not surprisingly he asked after his kinsman.

"Donnacona died," Cartier said. And then he told a lie: "But the others have married and live like great lords in France. They do not want to return."

Agona seemed satisfied. "I think," says the short narrative of the voyage, "he took it so well because he remained lord and governor of the country by the death of the said Donnacona." Agona's position as chief was now secure.

Cartier anchored three ships at the mouth of the Cap Rouge River and sent the other two back to France to report Roberval's non-arrival. Then he built two forts, one on the cliff and the other on the shore below. They planted wheat and cabbage, lettuce and turnip seeds. The colony was named Charlesbourg Royal.

Cartier revisited Hochelaga. He went up-river in two boats with the intention of finding

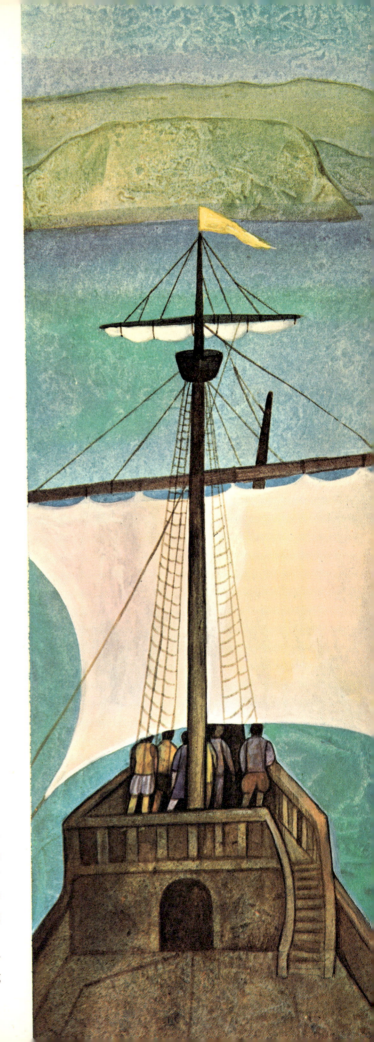

out more about the rapids that must be passed on the way to the Kingdom of Saguenay, which he hoped to visit in the spring. But he had no interpreters and learned very little.

When he returned to Charlesbourg Royal, Cartier found that the Indians were keeping away from the fort because they feared and mistrusted the Frenchmen. We do not know if they attacked Charlesbourg Royal for the narrative ends at this point. But it is not difficult to imagine that over the long winter the French-

men were discouraged by sickness and fear of the Indians. They gave up any thought of staying. The colony broke up and Cartier set sail in June. He was satisfied to leave because he possessed samples that might prove to be a fabulous discovery: a yellow mineral "as thick as a man's nail" that looked like gold, and stones that glistened like polished diamonds.

When the ships reached the harbour of St John's in Newfoundland, Cartier was confronted by Roberval who had just arrived with

his colonists. A brief contemporary account tells us Cartier

informed the General that he could not with his small company withstand the savages, which went about daily to annoy him, and that this was the cause of his return to France.

Roberval commanded him to go back to the St Lawrence. Cartier was unwilling. The Indians, he knew, would not welcome him and he was no doubt eager to show his new-found treasures to the king. So under cover of darkness he escaped from the harbour and Roberval's leadership and headed for France.

Roberval went on to Charlesbourg Royal. His colonizing attempt there was ruined by famine and scurvy — though it lasted until the following summer. (Little is said about the Indians, who were probably hostile.) When Roberval departed from the river, Canada was abandoned until the beginning of the next century.

Cartier's "gold and diamonds" met with sarcasm and mockery in France when it was discovered that they were nothing but iron pyrites and quartz. "Not worth a Canadian diamond" became a disdainful expression of the time. As far as we know Cartier did not go to sea again. He spent the rest of his life attending to the business of his manor-house, Limoilou, at St Malo. He died there in 1557.

Jacques Cartier discovered one of the great rivers of the world and he was the first man to survey the Gulf of St Lawrence and to describe the Indians who lived there and on the river. In the years ahead the St Lawrence would carry Frenchmen far afield over its tributary lakes and rivers — toward the Pacific? to China? They did not know. But in seeking to find out they would travel over three-quarters of the continent and lay claim to a vast colonial empire for France in North America.

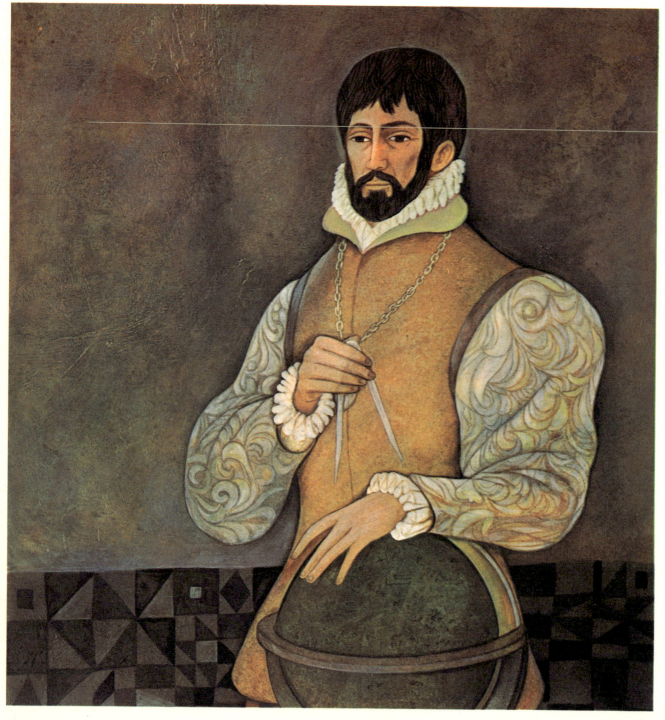

The text of this book is partly drawn from the same author's *The St Lawrence* (Oxford University Press).
The extracts are taken from *The Voyages of Jacques Cartier* translated and edited by H. P. Biggar.